# The G. Lie Hidden within Difficult Emotions

*Part 4: Disconnection and Loneliness*

Yuichi Handa, PhD

Book Layout ©2017 BookDesignTemplates.com
Cover Design by Islam Farid


The Gifts that Lie Hidden within Difficult Emotions (Part 4): Disconnection and Loneliness/ Yuichi Handa. -- 1st ed.
Printed in the United States of America
ISBN 13:9781090996930

# Table of Contents

## *Dedication*

To all of the people in my life who
have received me when I spoke my
truth, and who have spoken their
truth with me.  Also, to *Fuji-san!*

# 1 Brief autobiography

It used to be—and it could very well be in the future as well—that every once in a while, I would feel lonely, as if I were by myself in this world (at least among corporeal beings). My mind would survey the relational terrain of my life, and I would fail to see points of genuine connection. Or ones that felt reliable that I could count on.

And yet, this wasn't a feeling that arrived out of nowhere. It happened in response to a very specific set of internal stimuli. In other words, there was a cause that came from within. What that cause is will remain the mystery for the time being, to be revealed at length later in the book.

Instead for now, I hope to lead you, the reader, through a journey into loneliness and disconnection itself. From there, I hope to convince you how loneliness is a mental and emotional state that arises due to specific causes and conditions, much of which is about the choices we make and don't make, and that the experience of loneliness contains within itself its own "solution." That is, within loneliness is a gift that not only adds to our increasing repertoire of spiritual faculties, but provides us with a way of viewing and experiencing reality in such a way so as to experience it as one of continual connection and presence.

# 2 Starting point

Most everyone knows loneliness. And yet, I'll suggest that many truly don't.

We've all experienced it to varying degrees in our lives, and yet there's such a profound and prevalent aversion to the experience of it that many if not most of us haven't paused to examine the actual lived experience of loneliness and disconnection, and thus, the knowing and not knowing. I trace this partly to the fact that some of the most vocal among us are regularly cheering and advocating for connection and community. God forbid you're not feeling connected. Something must be wrong with you. Or so you're led to believe.

In a culture that prizes connection so highly, what gets pushed into the shadow of the collective psyche is loneliness, disconnection, and to some extent, even solitude. And when something gets pushed into the shadow, there's an associated shame around that experience and feeling. The result of the shame is that instead of examining and possibly even appreciating the object of shame, we tend to shirk away from it. We try fixing, denying, or ameliorating it as if it were a disease.

But instead, I want to convince you how it would be much better, pragmatically, if one were to take the attitude that it's okay to feel lonely and disconnected, that there's nothing to fix even if that may fly in the face of advice from many self-help books, blogs, experts, psychologists, and so on. But it's what I know to be true. Thinking that loneliness is wrong or defective doesn't help in any way that I'm aware of, and in fact, will worsen the situation, for one will be resisting one's experience as it is.

If you happen to be experiencing loneliness, then being with it and digesting it, can be one of the best things to do. There's no need to fix it. You needn't change your life around to avoid it, assuage it, or relieve yourself of it. Instead, why not accept it, even rejoice in it? Be happy for it. In fact, just a shade off from loneliness is yearning, and some of the greatest poetry and art from around the world arises from this particular state. Similarly, loneliness itself can give rise to much beauty in this world. This connection between the experience of loneliness and beauty is one that will be touched upon later.

If you've already learned to eat your confusion, stuckness, and lack, then disconnection is the fourth entrée in this five-course meal. It comes with the most precious and rarest of gifts (or rare wherever loneliness tends to be a bugaboo word). If you shun it, trying to manipulate the outsides in order to compensate *against* it—i.e., desperately seeking out or clinging to people or particular persons—you'll miss out on the deepest intimacies imaginable, and you'll end up back where you began anyways, back to loneliness and disconnection. And what would be the point of it other than to discover that you're capable of traveling in circles?

# 3 Loneliness and aloneness; disconnection and solitude

Many of us know that *aloneness* is different from *loneliness*, that we can be alone without feeling lonely or disconnected, and also, that we can be among many and still feel lonely and disconnected.

This book isn't about aloneness or solitude. It's about loneliness and disconnection.

I've heard it said that it's okay to be alone, that you needn't feel lonely just because you're alone. That may be true. *But the point of this book is that it's okay to feel lonely also. It's okay to feel disconnected also.* There's nothing wrong with these either.

This isn't about learning to be alone without feeling lonely. *It's about learning to be lonely without panicking about it.* It's about embracing loneliness and disconnection.  Not trying to escape it, fix it, or make it be anything other than how it is.

# 4 In praise of solitude, and on the role of loneliness

It's hard to enjoy solitude—that is, to relish the joys of aloneness—if there's resistance to experiencing loneliness because loneliness can be part of the experience of solitude. It can be like a gatekeeper to the true riches of solitude.

But also, some of us may have difficulty enjoying solitude because we don't have a meaningful sense of what that avails us. We know what having friends, family, and partners offers—company and companionship. We have enough bombardment of media and culture telling us the virtues of companionship, community, family, and so on. But some of us don't have a genuinely positive image of what having none of those around gives us (and no, it isn't hobbies, Netflix, books, and pets, although those can come too).

What can arise is an inner life, a *connection*, if you will, to an inner reality, to what the Greeks called the "Great Mystery." Some might call it "Spirit" or "God," and not just in concept but in actual experience. The names may differ, but the structure of experience appears common across most traditions. We become familiarized to an unseen and invisible reality that hides from view for many. We become able to discern the subtle threads that bind seemingly unrelated choices and situations. We become more attuned to the hidden mysteries of living. Intuition becomes a primary voice within. Coincidences and synchronicities arise with greater frequency. We begin to see our capacity for creativity grow, not because we magically become "creative" or artistic, but because we begin to notice what's being offered us from within and without in each moment. In short, we come to *decipher* (from *de* ("from") + *cipher* ("nothing, zero, naught," thus to make something from nothing) a kind of creative code, and thus, join the constant and continual creation of reality around us out of the great Void, the Great Mystery.

Loneliness then is the initiation into that great mystery—one of the primary gatekeepers. It's perhaps one of the more difficult mental and emotional states. If it were easy, everyone would be an oracle or prophet (as if they weren't already)!

# 5 Neediness, clinginess, and fantasyland

But what happens when you're bent on avoiding loneliness?

You can become needy. Instead of relishing your loneliness, your mind starts looking for ways to relieve that loneliness. One way in which it can do so is that it can start grasping at others, whether at friends or current and/or potential mates. In fact, the urge to finding a mate or staying in unfulfilling relationships and friendships, for some, could be rooted in an avoidance of loneliness. If that's so, there's nothing inherently wrong with it, but it could be limiting, as it could easily lead to settling for something that one doesn't truly cherish and embrace. But since it keeps loneliness at bay, it becomes easy to settle against one's values.

And what happens from there? Maybe a *fantasy* begins occupying the mind that one day the person will change, or that you'll change, or else that the relationship/friendship/partnership itself will change? And as the make-believe becomes more firmly entrenched in mind, reality recedes further and further until one day, you wake from your dream with the realization that you've spent years living in a fantasy. Of course, to live in such a fantasy would require staying in a state of denial and confusion. You'd likely suffer from a lack of clarity in your life, in which case you could go back and read the first book in this series. But be warned! If you read that book and start allowing space around you, you might find yourself unexpectedly waking from such a dream.

Or maybe you try emotionally manipulating your partner so that s/he better fits your desires. See how well that works (I've tried it). You're basically asking for more than that person can offer you. This shows up as neediness. You feel needy (and they call you needy) because you keep seeking what's not coming. You're trying to squeeze orange juice out of an apple. So you stay thirsty (needy).

Maybe you try changing the other through regular complaints for not meeting your "needs." It's a kind of control. You can request something of another, but if it's not forthcoming, then it's not forthcoming. It's up to you to keep trying to change the other, or for you to let it go. But maybe you don't let go. Why? Because you'd have to confront your loneliness, that state of feeling disconnected.

Or maybe you don't do any of that. Meanwhile, you settle for something your heart isn't fully aligned with. All in the name of avoiding loneliness, you stay in something that doesn't connect to your deepest being. And you struggle in it. And you're willing to give up your ties to reality to remain in this fantasyland.

Or maybe you change your partner by exchanging him or her with another? That's something altogether different, but it's got the same needy undertone. So you end up single while seeking another partner, but anyone *of value* would smell the stink of neediness in you from a mile away. So you'd have to settle again for someone not quite in line with what you would truly choose. And that's just one of the possible paths available to you for avoiding loneliness.

# 6 Expectations

Another word for *need*iness is expectations. We sometimes form expectations of others and/or of situations that they work out in a way that would somehow meet, even fulfill our "needs."

It's reasonable to communicate what we consider our needs, but then *expecting* that they be met by the recipient of our expressed needs is problematic. Either the person or persons meet our needs or they don't. Either they choose to do so or they won't. How you choose to respond from there will be shaped at least in part by your relationship to loneliness. If you have a comfortable relationship to it, then you'll either patiently give it some time (during which you may experience a kind of emotional or mental disconnection from that person) or else move on until things change for the better (which may involve a more complete disconnection associated with parting). If you do neither, then you'll likely stay dissatisfied while being filled with unmet expectations, either withering away in hopelessness or festering in resentment.

# 7 A distinction from lack

Although neediness can appear like a feeling of lack as explored in part three of this series, there exists a subtle distinction between the two. Certainly, the two can overlap and coexist, but they're not identical.

Lack requires no outward reference whereas neediness occurs in relation to some *other*. While lack *can* show up in our relationships, it can also show up as an intrinsic state, whereas neediness is a condition embedded in one's feelings and experiences of connectedness and disconnectedness to other, whether that other is another human being, an animal, a flower, or a deity.

The obsession for a mind caught in lack is *more,* as in "one more drink" or "one more thing to buy." The obsession for a mind wrapped up in loneliness and neediness is *connection,* as in wanting "a connection to feeling alive" (that for example, some drugs and most forms of social media provide) or "a connection to another." Using video games, television, Netflix, internet, Facebook, porn, and so on, in an addictive manner oftentimes is an attempt to create some kind of connection, whether to fictional characters, to virtual friends, to disembodied others, and so on. It's less about compensating for lack, as in wanting more (although that can be there too).

Even though both lack and disconnection can show up as addiction in our culture, the underlying dynamic can be distinguished. Of course, many who suffer from one suffer from the other.

For example, consider workaholism. If it's motivated by a feeling of lack, then it's usually accompanied by a drive for *more* money, status, prestige, and/or power. It's to fill a hole inside.

But if that same workaholism is motivated more by a compulsion to avoiding loneliness or the resulting neediness, then it's acting more as a *distraction*. You stay in the office till late because you don't want to deal with the loneliness that will ensue when you leave. As long as you're busy, you're not feeling disconnected. And yet, the distraction of busyness is what sustains your sense of disconnection. Your busyness speaks of your own feelings of disconnection. In other words, *the seeking of and immersion into distractions can be thought of as an integral and essential part of the experience of disconnection and loneliness.*

# 8 Unpacking distraction

When you consider that the etymology of the word
*distract* comes from the Latin *distractus* (meaning to
"draw away," from *dis-* ("away") + *-trahere* ("to draw")),
the invisible thread connecting our habits of distraction to
a psyche that would draw away from *what is,* from things
as they are, becomes revealed.  That is, *our drive to
distraction is at the heart of the disconnecting act.*

When we feel lonely and disconnected, we perpetuate our
disconnection through seeking distraction.  They're one
and the same psychological process.  In fact, one could
say that disconnection and loneliness come about through
the seeking of distractions, or drawing away from.
  Another way to say it is this: our seeking of distractions
reveals to us our own disconnection.

Many of us fill our lives with countless distractions,
situations, and activities that we know hold little intrinsic
value for us (including dissatisfying relationships)—
sometimes leading us into needy or compulsive patterns
of behavior.  And why might we be doing this?  It's
usually because *there's a resistance to being with things*

*as they are.*  But if we've been distracting ourselves for most of our lives, that means that we've been disconnecting from things as they are for much of that time, which means that our resultant experience of things as they truly are is likely one of disconnection.  Therefore, in order to restore some sense of connection, we have to connect with our own feelings of disconnection, more commonly called loneliness.

It's a bit of a paradox, isn't it, that *the path of connection runs through our feelings of disconnection and loneliness?*

To repeat, when you've buried your life in distractions, your internal reality is that you're feeling disconnected.  So, one of the most viable experiences for you to connect to is your own disconnection.  You drop your propensity toward distractions by embracing your own disconnected state, which is just another way of saying that you open up to your loneliness.  That is, you eat it.

# 9 Co-dependence

Suppose a person didn't have an aversion to loneliness and disconnection. Suppose instead that she relished the experience of loneliness as much as she might relish the experience of joy, love, and happiness.

Would she be capable of staying in co-dependent arrangements within her relationships?

Likely not. She would be willing to bring more authenticity and integrity into her relationships, even at the cost of potentially losing the relationship itself and ending up feeling forlorn and abandoned in the process, all of which pass but in an instant *if allowed to be.*

# 10 The troubles with lists

A common suggestion for a person in a codependent relationship is to suggest that the person exit such a relationship so that they can find a better relationship. So, go from feeble connection to a robust connection. But it rarely works that way.

If you exit one codependent relationship, you usually end up in another one. Wherever you go, there you are, as the saying goes. You recreate the same dynamics but simply change the scenery and the props (the other person). In this way, exiting may be the expedient solution, but not always an effective one. (What may be a more effective solution will be discussed at length later in the book. For now, the focus is on the troubles.)

Or maybe, in the name of more realistic thinking, a person decides to buttress his desires against a long make-or-break list of traits that one looks for in potential partners as if one's heart and life were decided on paper. Even if one were to encounter such a candidate, we'd likely get into the "S/he's perfect on paper, but…" phenomenon. The heart isn't into it.

Erecting a list can sometimes be a subtle ploy to keep from confronting one's inherent aloneness, as if the motivation behind it were, "If the person meets all of my needs and desires (read demands), it'll somehow work out and I won't end up in this lonely place again." A list can act as a protective mechanism against disappointment and heartbreak. And why would averting heartbreak matter? Because heartbreak might mean returning to loneliness and disconnection.

Heartbreak in and of itself is little more than a tender, painful feeling in the heart. It's not the end of things. In fact, it can feel as if we're connecting to an inherent sadness to living, as it can stand in for all the partings that we endure as part of the human experience. In this way, it can even feel poignantly beautiful at times. Heartbreak oftentimes isn't the problem. It's the accompanying feelings of loneliness, clinging, and hopelessness that many of us find much more of a struggle.

On the other hand, if you were at ease in your loneliness and disconnection, why would you care about some list? You would meet each person as they presented themselves to you, not whether they accorded with some list that you set *a priori* to an encounter. You would meet them *freshly* with your heart, not with a stale list (stale as in reified from the past, and not current and moving with the ever-unfolding present moment). *And you would trust the discernment of your own heart in the moment.* There would not be the need for such self-protection because you would trust your own capacity at discerning what was obviously going to be a problem for you in the moment while also being open to what may and may not change in the future.

# 11 Another problem with lists

The other complication with make-or-break lists is they're oftentimes based upon our preferences, which happen to be based entirely on past experiences and programming, meaning we're trying to recreate and relive our past. We won't be flinging ourselves into a wide-open future. Instead, we'll be limiting possibilities.

If we're going to have a list, we would do better to have it be littered with eternal principles, such as generosity, compassion, kindness, and the like. And then, learn to embody those principles ourselves. We don't need a list to put upon someone else. We need one for ourselves. In other words, we can focus on our own growth as human beings, and in time, we'll naturally find ourselves surrounded with like-minded people *for the most part.*

Needless to say, this brief discussion on lists is applicable not just to romantic partners, but to work partners, workout partners, friendships, and so on.

End of story (on lists).

# 12 An alternative to codependency

So, what would be an alternative to settling for a less-than-genuinely-desired set of relationships? It's to seek out *genuine* connections. Not palliatives, or company just to distract us from our loneliness. But *real* connection.

It's not always a clear distinction between authentic relationship and a counterfeit kind of association that helps us mostly to forget our loneliness but little more. We can easily get lost in relationships that simply are a distraction away from what may be an intrinsic disconnection to the universe and to life. *To distinguish or to discern the difference is paramount in fostering meaningful connections.*

Without such discrimination or sensitivity of heart, we're either left to settle for less than what our hearts would seek, or get caught up managing and erecting lists, rules, and expectations until we're so tight and closed off that there's little chance of a genuine and sustaining connection to another, and more importantly, to life itself.

And so, where does this discernment of heart and mind arise?

It comes out of acknowledging, welcoming, and embracing—that is, opening up to and digesting—our loneliness, and extracting out this most precious of capacities from it!

# 13 Why the resistance?

And yet, many of us turn away from loneliness. Why might that be?

A lot of it might have to do with our cultural programming. There's *tremendous* pressure to be connected, whether it be in the form of family and friends, or virtually, through social media websites and the like. It's as if there's something wrong to feel disconnected. Even people who disconnect online give reasons that prioritize deeper and further connections offline. It's not uncommon to hear, "I'm signing off on my Facebook account so that I can honor my real-life relationships." Basically, they're saying, "I give up this less meaningful form of connection for a deeper or more authentic form of connection." And yet, you rarely if ever hear people say, "I'm going to sign off on Facebook so that I can be by myself more and explore and enjoy my loneliness and utter disconnectedness to life."

In short, there's tremendous resistance to disconnection built into our primary tribe, which is our culture. It somehow is taken as "wrong" or "unhealthy." And yet, we often don't stop to question: if I'm feeling lonely right now, isn't that the reality of the situation? And if that's how it is, wouldn't it make sense to embrace it for what it is rather than trying to deny or overcome it? And really, *isn't the act of embracing an experience that's happening in the moment an act of connecting to reality as it is?*

In other words, embracing whatever is happening in the moment—no matter how unpleasant—is the most immediate way of connecting to Life as a whole (and not just to one or a few human beings). And if the current experience happens to be the state of loneliness, then the relating to and allowing of that loneliness may be the actual path toward connection. *If the heart of loneliness is an experience of disconnection, embracing that loneliness is precisely the path toward its own fulfillment as well as to its undoing.*

Stated more generally, if one is in darkness, why spend time and energy despairingly looking for the light that appears absent at the moment? Why not instead appreciate and more fully enter the darkness? Light comes of its own accord. One needn't seek it or look for it. It arises of itself, and the best we can do is not to interfere with its arrival.

Trying to avoid and overcome darkness when it's dark is a bit like panicking because it's night time. Instead, we can rest (our hearts and minds), *trusting* that light will come again at day break. In this way, we remain connected to phenomenal reality.

*It's the denial of the darkness that disconnects us, not the darkness itself.*

# 14 What resides within loneliness and disconnection?

When we actually stop to allow for loneliness and disconnection to be, we can become curious about it. We can explore its textures. And if we go deeply enough into it, we can begin to see into its nature.

It's helpful to contrast loneliness with aloneness here. Whereas the former usually arises along with a certain angst and anxiety, the latter—without the accompanying loneliness—can be a peaceful state.

This begs the question: What makes loneliness more anxiety-ridden than aloneness?

When you sit with your loneliness and carefully examine it, you might soon notice an underlying graspiness. When we're lonely, we're usually seeking and/or grasping at something. We're looking for a connection that's not forthcoming, and thus, we're left with the experience we call loneliness. In contrast, when we're simply alone, we're not looking outwardly in that manner. We may simply be engaged in an activity or enjoying the pleasures of being without seeking for connection with a specific other.

Think of a time in your life when you were alone but not lonely, for example, when you were on your own on a trip, and there was a sense of promise, hope, excitement, and maybe even peace. Now contrast that with a time when you felt a profound sense of loneliness or disconnection. What's the difference?

Can you notice it's not the external conditions that determine your loneliness? Can you recognize the graspy, clingy, needy qualities inherent within the experience of loneliness? It's not what's happening on the outside that's inherent to loneliness. Those outside events (or non-events) may trigger some grasping, which then becomes your loneliness. But it's not these outside events that we call loneliness. It's what gets triggered, and that's the conditioning of the heart and mind that clutches, that grasps.

If you're without that clutching, then there's peace. Then, it's simply that you're alone. It's that you have solitude, and you have an opportunity to enjoy, even relish your lovely solitude. But *with* the clinginess, there's no peace. *So, it's this clinging and grasping that sits near the heart of loneliness and disconnection.* Not the fact that there's no one around, for we're always connected whether we like it or not, whether we feel it or not. But somehow the grasping moves us toward feelings of disconnection. *The grasping is our loneliness.*

A question then arises—What might be at the root of our grasping?

# 15 Craving

Rather than think of it as grasping, it might help to think of it as a craving—or more precisely, an unsatiated craving, to be distinguished from plain hunger. Hunger corresponds to a lack (from part 3 of this series), which again implies a need for *more*. On the other hand, a craving is pinpoint specific. We don't crave just any food. While practically anything will do with hunger, it's the specific object of our desire that we're after with craving.

And so, the kind of grasping we're looking at is more along the lines of a craving. It's that we're grasping for something and not finding it. That's loneliness. That's disconnection.

But then, what underlies—that is, gives rise to and supports—such craving?

# 16 Looking for fulfillment in all the wrong places

If you look carefully, what you may find is that craving is fueled by a desire that's not being allowed expression. The desire isn't wrong in itself. We could even call such a desire a yearning. *Not all yearnings need be fulfilled. But they require expression.* They need, for lack of a better term, space within which they can *be* so that they can run their *true* course, whatever shape and form that may take. Sometimes that course is simply toward dissipation. Other times, it's toward a concrete end. But we don't always know what that end is. The desire itself does.

And yet with craving, the same desire is being hemmed in, trapped, not out of an intention to suffocate it, but in our failure to allow it to be, so as to reveal its true nature. In this way, the desire is being *misdirected* in a way that subtly disregards it, leaving it unexpressed (and here, I don't mean that one has to vocalize one's desire, but rather, the desire isn't being allowed its natural expression however that may be). The misdirection often comes

from a lack of patience, of acting too soon before the
desire has fully made itself clear.

It's not that different from acting out on anger.  If we
speak out or act in the midst of anger, we oftentimes don't
obtain the desired results compared to sitting through the
anger and processing it, and speaking/acting only when
we've reached a level of clarity around the issue at hand.
Same with desire.  We can sit with it and allow it to be.
We can process it until we're at ease and peace, and can
then act with clarity.

Can you see the underlying issue here?  *We're defaulting
to what may be an expedient solution when desire herself
may seek something much deeper, larger, and more
authentic; and because we've chosen the quick and easy
path, there's little fulfillment to the desire and yearning,
which in turn shows up as unabated desire, or craving.*

The easy (or quick) answer fails to fulfill.  We seemingly
end up with disappointment after disappointment, failing
to see that *the cause rests in our expediency,* and not in
what's out there.  As the saying goes, we find ourselves
looking for love (or connection) in all the wrong places,
or in all the wrong ways.

# 17 Choosing based upon expediency

Have you ever been in an intimate relationship where you live with somebody, or else you go on a trip with that person, and you experience such excruciating loneliness even though you're sleeping in the same bed with that other? There's a longing and desire for genuine connection that's not being met, which results in a sense of neediness and loneliness. Or profound disconnection. But you can also be alone, filled with a longing that's also unmet that can lead to a similar feeling of loneliness and disconnection.

In each of these instances, we've somehow put ourselves in a place where we're craving for some connection, and yet, the underlying desire for it isn't being met, leading our minds to becoming graspy.

In such instances, we could say that we've made a series of choices that have caused us to end up there. If you think back on the discussion on distraction, we've likely made our choices not for authentic and genuine connection but rather for associations that would distract us away from the inherent disconnection and/or aloneness we were already experiencing. Again, due to our expediency, we may have chosen a relationship or set of relationships as distractions—or we may have made choices *within* our relationships that embody distractedness or busyness[1]—rather than as a deepening or a pursuit of *true* intimacy.

And so, our whole life on some level has been built as a drawing away, as a disconnecting, and in turn, our relationships have become the manifest representations of the disconnectedness of our *choices*.

---

[1] For example, one could argue that frequent messaging in our close relationships, while sometimes acting as a substitute for meaningful engagement, more often affords a kind of disengaged engagement. It creates the appearance of connection while in fact calling upon us to bring very little of ourselves in such interactions, as it rests upon our own *convenience* to engage. It doesn't require a commitment of time (such as would a lunch date or phone call) or the development of skills in navigating the complexities of an in-person dialogue (which include learning how to gracefully exit such encounters). In this way, messaging and texting can become the medium of choice for those whose minds are busily *distracted* in a multitude of tasks, unready and/or unwilling to settle into meaningful engagement.

# 18 Two e-words related to expediency

*"Our being is not to be enriched merely by activity and experience as such. Everything depends on the quality of our acts and our experiences. A multitude of badly performed actions and of experiences only half-lived exhausts and depletes our being. By doing things badly we make ourselves less real. The growing unreality cannot help but make us unhappy... There are times, then, when in order to keep ourselves in existence at all we simply have to sit back for a while and do nothing... We must first recover the possession of our own being."*
— Thomas Merton

We live in a culture where time feels short. Many of us are *busy* with our lives. If you browse the nonfiction section of a bookstore, you'll find numerous books on time management. What many of us are striving for within the game of living well is *efficiency*. We carry around our smartphones so that we can accomplish (mostly menial) tasks when we're out and about. We learn to multitask, even to the point of utter inefficiency. But the underlying motivation is efficiency.

What's lost in the shuffle of efficiency is *effectiveness.* Accomplishing one hundred tasks in a day may provide us with a sense of efficiency in living, but we may not be effective at anything—that is, we may not be causing a meaningful and sustaining *effect* upon our lives, our well-being, the well-being of others, the well-being of the planet, and so on.

It's not necessarily one or the other. But I also wouldn't argue for a balance between the two.

Instead, I would suggest that a life based more so on effectiveness will find its own efficiency, whereas the other way around usually doesn't happen. Better to do one thing well in a day than 100 things unsoundly. Better to have internalized and embodied two or three passages from a single book through repeated readings than to have superfluously read 50 books with little residue! ;)

Expediency is a mindset that associates with efficiency. If you find yourself choosing expediency in relation to your desires and yearnings, you might examine the rest of your life and see how much efficiency you strive for, or how little you pause to consider genuine effectiveness (which might be on par with meaningfulness) in your day-to-day living. The former requires little deliberation. The latter requires living reflectively and thoughtfully; it requires slowing things down. Not as an expedient solution, but as a way of being, or as a way of life.

# 19 **Approach one:** being with our yearning

Some of us choose expediency in regards to desire because we don't think to abide with our desire itself. We don't think to allow for it to be. Instead, we seek an outlet or fulfillment to our desire *prematurely* without close examination of its own nature.

And yet, what would it mean to abide with desire itself? What does that even look like?

It means honoring and feeling our yearnings. It means being with our yearning without a compulsion toward *acting* upon it. We simply remain with it without any rush toward its fulfillment. As implied earlier, it's not very different from sitting with anger, at least in the mechanics of it. And yet, honoring our yearning has a different tone than being with our anger.

Some of the most beautiful poetry, such as by Neruda, Machado, the Japanese haiku poets, and so on, are studies in yearning. Not as a guide toward their fulfillment, but as an honoring of a noble state of being with its own intrinsic beauty.  The poet Robert Bly has remarked that we live in a culture that doesn't know how to feel and honor the emotion of yearning.  And yet, this is what it means to abide with desire.  It's to abide with our yearning.  Not to seek to fulfill it, but to allow for it to be, and for it to find its own natural (as in non-manipulated) course of expression

When we don't allow ourselves to yearn, what happens?  We set ourselves at odds with our own hearts.  Our hearts intrinsically long and yearn, and yet, we aren't allowing for it.  Because we're now at odds with our own hearts, we draw to us those that reflect this fundamental split we have with our own hearts, as our relationship with others is many times (always) reflective of our own relationship to our own hearts.

Yet, if we were to remain with our yearning without seeking its fulfillment so readily, we might hear its *true* fulfillment.  That is, *we might discern its innermost calling.*  We will have allowed for desire to find its natural expression, it's intrinsic flow.  In turn, we wouldn't be caught in grasping, for the desire would have run its course, its natural fulfillment, and many times, its natural dissipation.  And without the grasping, there wouldn't be the experience of loneliness—aloneness and solitude perhaps, but not the clinging and craving of loneliness.

In this way, *it's the lack of discernment to hearing desire's innermost calling that characterizes loneliness and disconnection.*

By eating and being with our loneliness, we're led to listen past the outer sheaths of our desire all the way to its innermost aspect. We learn to remain with our desire until it speaks its most intimate and secret truths to us. That's the gift in staying with and eating loneliness.

Easier said than done of course. But as I've written in a prior book, we're not asked to do this in one sitting. We can take it in, one bite at a time. And each bite counts. Each time we slow down to feel desire as it presents itself to us without the rush toward action, we move that much closer to understanding its deeper calling.

# 20 Connecting to the divine

A desire for a love interest can *sometimes* be the outer casing of a deeper desire for connection with life itself. In Christianity, there is the idea that all yearning is simply a cover for the desire for union with God. In a more general sense, much of our deepest yearning for connection may be a yearning for connection to the divine however that may manifest in one's life—whether in a religious sense, through nature, through an inner stillness, and so on.

I won't argue that it's universal or applicable in all situations because I don't believe it is. But for most of us, there's a hunger and thirst for something more than our ordinary reality. Even the use of "spirits" or recreational drugs is many times undergirded by a pull toward something more, something deeper—although perhaps it's the expedient choice in many cases. I simply use the word "divine" to stand in as an umbrella term for something beyond the veil of ordinary reality and consciousness where there may be an accompanied tone of the sacred, profound, or mysterious and mystical.

If we examine our yearning for connection with another, it may truly be a social or bodily impulse, but other times, we can find that it's a substitute for something deeper. And when we recognize it as such and begin to honor that—that is, allow for the hunger and thirst for this most profound of yearnings to be and to express itself as it naturally would—something in us begins to settle. That is, we shed a restlessness that's continuously peeking out into a future or wrestling in remorse over a past. We lose a restless *distractedness* that seeks fulfillment from without; and the fulfillment, if one can call it that, comes to be. There's now nowhere to turn for anything more. We *come to rest* in the present.

Coming to rest in the present is a different experience from *striving* to become present, to mentally coercing our attention in the present. The latter is an efforting while the former is about settling in, from our heart, into the moment. One could call it an effortless presence as opposed to an effortful one. In the former, the heart settles into its own restfulness. It's no longer a seeking but a "being found" in the eternal moment.

And our practice, if we desire one, becomes to rest and remain in this.

This is one fruition—possibly the deepest kind—of working through our clinging and attachment, through loneliness and neediness. We find that our so-called need of a connection "out there" was simply a misdirected or misgauged impulse. Our miss wasn't one of impulse but of aim: of mistaking the image from the projector. We simply stopped short at the object of our desire. We didn't persist *through* that object toward the Source, which would have been the heart of Life itself, but also toward our innermost heart, where upon arrival, we can sometimes discover these to be one and the same. That is, we come to experience the collapse of common conceptual boundaries such as inside and outside, within and without, self and Life/God. We begin to suspect or even come to understand that there may not be the solid distinctions we imagined, that these were false dichotomies. They were simply conceptual overlays upon reality that we mentally agreed upon at some point and held up in our minds, and that in fact, there can be no meaningful separation from what lies deep in our hearts and what lies deep in the will of the universe (God). There was only one will, one desire, that of union, of utter interdependence and the loss of separation.

Here is the true fruition.

And naturally, our distractedness settles. We've arrived—although only temporarily for most of us—at the heart of connection.

# 21 Not the rule

And yet, I offer the last section as a possibility only. I don't make the claim that all desire and yearning for connection is a guise for connection to the divine. Sometimes it fits, and other times, seeing *through* what presents itself to us, this transcendence, can be a denial of things as they are. And such denial is a suppression of and aversion to reality, which rarely if ever truly supports our peace.

In other words, the impulse toward transcendence can sometimes be a rejection of things as they are. And other times, it's what's true in our hearts. The question becomes, how do we know which is which?

In short, we know by the result. If the result is real peace, then that becomes the mark of what's true for our hearts. Relief, or liberation, is the result we seek. As the saying goes, "The truth shall set you free."

# 22 A self-betrayal

*"How we do one thing is how we do everything."*
*—Anonymous*

What happens then when we don't stay true to our heart's innermost yearnings, when our choices are based upon expediency rather than calling?

In short, there's a kind of self-betrayal going on. Maybe we choose a career based less upon genuine passion and love, and more for the feeling of security and stability it seemingly promises? And maybe for a select few, security is the passion (although that sounds strange just in writing it)? For most of us, security is the safety net, not the passion. It's not the heart's real calling.

Or we do the same with a partner, or our friendships. It doesn't matter the area of life. If we're doing it somewhere, it's likely going to show up elsewhere, as there's no such thing as a compartment of one's life. It's simply one life, not even our own. Just life, singular, communally shared.

So, if we're betraying our own hearts in career choice, for example, then the same sort of choosing will invariably show up in the people we surround ourselves with. Similarly, if we're forsaking our heart's deepest yearnings in *how* we choose to interact with a partner, that same manner of choosing *will* show up elsewhere in our lives. This is only because *there's a common denominator across all situations and contexts for each of us, and that's our mind with its selfsame tendencies and habits.* Thus, the saying: how we do one thing is how we do everything.

When we fail to live from our core, we might rationalize it. And yet, most of us know when this is happening, whether within ourselves or in others. We can sense the difference in tone. When it's true, we can feel the heart in it. But when rationalizing, there's little to no heart. And this same want of heart shows up elsewhere in our lives or in the others'. And when the heart is continually left wanting, we *will* experience disconnection as we'll be disconnected from our own hearts.

"Neediness" then is another word for having lost touch with an essential aspect of ourselves. It derives from abandoning our own heart. The greater the abandonment, the less natural contentment we'll experience and the more we'll look for something or someone outside of us to remedy this state of affairs, which we call neediness.

In this way, neediness points to a lack of discernment in our choices, which is another way of saying that we were untrue in our choosing.

When we betray our own hearts, others can also betray us in similar ways. That is, we open ourselves up to the deception of others through our own subtle self-deceit.

As such, betrayal can be seen as a gift, as painful as it may be in the moment. It can be a call back toward re-examining our own manner of choosing, or stated more bluntly, it's a last resort measure of life itself, helping us to wake up to the untrueness and undiscerning manner of how we choose.

If we want to stay abreast (or even ahead?) of life so that such harsh awakenings aren't required of us, a useful question worth asking regularly is: *where and in what areas of my life might there be a self-betrayal going on?*

# 23 The opposite of loneliness

If the heart of disconnection is a graspiness arising out of misguided choices, then the opposite of loneliness and disconnection isn't company and connection. *It's discernment—or, the emergence of the discerning heart.* It's what space is to confusion, what clarity is to stuckness, what equanimity is to lack. It's what you want to aim for when you're lonely. You don't go for company or connection when you're lonely. You seek out greater discernment—that is, the capacity to distinguish true from false, real from illusory. You look toward your heart's intrinsic wisdom.

Ultimately, this is how you can arrive at genuine and meaningful connection, through the cultivation, or unearthing of the *heart* that discerns. This is the gift of eating loneliness and disconnection, the signpost that lets you know that you are in fact digesting your disconnection.

If you attempt to go from disconnection to connection without discernment, you may still find yourself with less loneliness, temporarily, but either without *genuine* connection (which is to say you've basically distracted yourself), or if you're feeling connected *to others*, you may have abandoned connection to yourself.

This is why we can sometimes feel even lonelier by seeking out certain types of company—the wrong type for us, usually the kind where we're not quite able to be open and honest around them. And this is why seeking out community and connection without the cultivation and practice of discernment fails to resolve the original state of disconnection. It fails to recognize the direction in which our loneliness and disconnection must be transformed—not toward connection itself, but toward the heart that discerns.

## 24 Food metaphor

I've noticed an interesting thing around food. After
consuming a large and *empty* meal, I'm often not so
hungry for my next meal. Recently, I ate five large slices
of pizza along with a coke and pie for dinner. The next
day, I didn't feel hungry till evening. It's as if my
stomach was telling me, "I don't like the shit you toss
down here! I'm going to shut down for a while!"

I think the same goes for our relationships. When we
choose our friends and companions without
discernment—or that our manner of interacting with them
lacks discernment—something in us rebels and closes
down. It's as if our hearts say, "You aren't exposing me to
the right kinds of people or interacting in a meaningful
way even with the right people. I'm now going to be a
little less excited about human interactions."

If we aren't diligent about practicing some measure of
discernment in how we relate with others, we can end up
with an emotional brand of malnutrition. That is, if we
continue to shove "unhealthy," "non-nutritious"
relationships or manners of relating down our emotional
gullet, we'll get more and more heart upset, and in turn,

close down for further engagement and interaction. In short, we become inclined to isolate ourselves from others.

And yet, this is exactly the condition of loneliness and neediness. Our lack of discernment and discrimination has caused something within us to shut down from further reaching out and connecting. We end up lonely.

# 25 Detached discernment

True discernment requires detachment, for an underlying graspiness will muddy one's capacity at settling out the true from the false. I know, for example, that when I'm single and I meet an attractive woman, my capacity at discerning that person's character is often compromised, at least for a short while. It's because I've lost detachment—that is, I'm attached now to an outcome.

As long as we're *clinging* to some hope of a particular end result, we'll fail to discern what's in front of us, or what's availing itself to us. If your goal is to distinguish what's true from what's not, then holding onto and attempting to assert your own agenda (driven by your attachments) will only muddy the waters. Becoming detached from—not in denial of—self-concern will help in sussing out the true from the false.

But to a large extent, that was the content of book 3, where the focus was on establishing equanimity as an even, impartial, and flat mind. This equanimity is the detachment that's required of real discernment.

And yet, it's not enough for discernment. Equanimity/detachment is a precondition but not an equivalence.

## 26 **Approach two:** discernment through *via negativa*

> "How do you sculpt an elephant?"
> "You chip away at all that isn't the elephant."
> —Anonymous

All this talk of discerning our heart's true desires might sound imposing. If you're one of the select people who knows what they really desire, that's a blessing. But what if you're not?

I've already suggested one way of coming closer to our heart's deepest impulses, and that's in honoring the mental/emotional state of yearning, and learning to abide within it with a detachment to outcome. We *inhabit* our yearning while concurrently *inhibiting* the compulsion toward acting upon it. Many times, acting upon an emotion is a way of not feeling it. So by inhibiting the urge toward action, we more fully remain with the experience of the emotion.

In this way, feeling our yearning and staying with it is a direct method toward coming into our heart's calling. But there is also an indirect approach: part of knowing what's in our hearts is knowing what's not. Some of us are good at this. We don't know exactly what we desire, but we're confident in knowing what we don't.

In daily life, this tendency can show up in rather mundane ways. For example, we may not be able to articulate what restaurant we want to go to with our friend, but we're very clear on where we *don't* want to eat. That's helpful information in the decision-making venture if we can understand that that's our contribution in the process. Or we may not know what movie we want to see, but we know which ones we don't. And so on.

This is *via negativa*, which comes from a theological attitude that God can't be known directly, but rather indirectly through knowledge of what He/She/It isn't. It's a viable path and method that can lead to true fruition when practiced with rigorous honesty, both with self and with others.

Being very honest with ourselves about what's not working and becoming willing to change or to let go (or to acknowledge and possibly express that truth for us) trims away in one form or another that which no longer resonates for us. As we do so, *we allow what may be true to come to the forefront.* That is, when we shed or release an aspect of our lives that's no longer heartfelt for us, something relaxes—whether in us or around us—and things begin to move; they begin to flow. We may still be incapable of consciously acknowledging what it is that we truly desire, but oftentimes what can happen instead is that things materialize that we recognize as exactly what we desired all along. We don't find, but we become found into a new life.

We don't always need to know what we truly want. *Many times, the most precious and important things to our hearts are without definition.* We can instead work with what we know to *not* be that. And as we release these things from our psyche and our lives, we draw closer and closer to an unknown fulfillment until something from the other side reaches out toward us, appears as if by magic, or by providence. And we recognize that the desire and yearning for it was in us all along even if we never knew so until its arrival.

# 27 Hell yes/no

In the spirit of *via negativa*, I'd like to mention a book I adore. It's called *Hell Yes: Two Little Words for a Happier, Simpler Life* by Elizabeth Baskin. It's a simple yet powerful book whose premise I can summarize in a few sentences.

Whenever you're confronted with a choice, ask yourself if it's a "hell yes" or something else. If it's anything other than a hell yes—including a moderate yes, a hesitant yes, or a later yes—then turn it into a hell no. Choose only those things that are outright hell yeses. Very simple. We put aside those endeavors and pursuits that don't make our hearts sing immediately in the present.

Imagine living a life based upon this heuristic. At first, it may seem as if you would choose nothing. Or that's how it felt to me initially. It felt rather nihilistic. It meant that I spent a lot of time doing little, mostly waiting. (I still do.) And yet, in time, I began to notice that I had hell yeses. And I began living them.

Or if I had a moderate yes, I asked myself the question, "Is there anything I can do to make this into a hell yes," and sometimes, there were ways to do so with only a small change in attitude or variation in approach.

Living a life of hell yeses can be frightening, but also exhilarating!  It's a simple way of bringing one's choices closer to that of a life lived from the heart.

# 28 On manifestation

Since I frequently come across the popular idea of manifesting, I'd like to add my own two cents on it within this discussion on discernment.

One thing is patently clear to me. We manifest constantly. It's impossible not to. It doesn't require belief, superstition, or any special powers. It's just a matter of fact. For example, if you've had a meal, you manifested that meal into your life. If you've spoken with anyone, you've manifested that encounter. If you've watched television or read a book, you manifested that show or book into your life. If you're laying down on a couch doing nothing, then you've manifested that experience as well. This is manifestation. If I want to manifest a lunch with a friend, I call up a friend and ask if he wants to have lunch. If he says he can't, then I call someone else. Eventually, I'm having lunch with a friend. In many ways, manifestation is nothing special. We're always doing it.

If it sounds ordinary, then it simply means that the mind is preoccupied with the ordinary, the everyday, and so what would one expect otherwise? If one wants to manifest the extraordinary, then one's focus has to be on the extraordinary. If one wants to manifest one's most heartfelt desires, then the focus has to be on that!

For many of us, our minds are confined in pursuit of security and certainty while out of touch with our deepest desires and yearnings. So we expend this wondrous capacity on accomplishing—that is, "manifesting"—for results of little to no consequence to ourselves.

Imagine having a wish-fulfilling jewel—a gem that we wish anything upon, and that wish comes true—and creating the life we desire. And yet, that's exactly how this thing works. Life *is* a wish-fulfilling jewel. We place a wish, and we create what we wish.[2]

We all have a capacity for creating a wondrous reality around us, and yet, most of us content ourselves with so little: mostly security and stability in an ever insecure and unstable world. What a profound waste!

So, the issue isn't whether we can manifest or not.

The issue is *where* our minds and hearts are pointed. If we don't take the time to tap into the heart's innermost yearnings, we'll be wasting away our lives creating a life of little to no consequence for ourselves.

---

[2] Naturally, we want to heed the age-old admonition, *be careful what you wish for!* While we may have a desire for a million dollars, for most of us, that's just a wish for security. And in my experience and observation, it's the insecure mind that seeks security, not the heart. Put simply, my heart has never spoken to me, *I want more money!* Or, *I require security!* And so on.

And how do we do things differently?

This is exactly the practice of discernment. As I've suggested, one way is through patient abiding with one's yearning, and the other, is through thoughtful and (again) patient application of *via negativa* to our choices. *Part of staying focused on what matters to us is in learning to say no to all the things that don't.* If we don't disengage from those things that our hearts aren't enlivened by, it'll feel as if we're wasting away our days, as if we're frittering away this tremendous capacity at (co)-creating a reality in line with our heart's deepest truths and yearnings.

# 29 A few more words on manifestation: still via negativa

Here's a warning—but an exciting one!

When we abide in our heart's yearnings, things do begin to show up. But not always what we think. Sometimes, what shows up at first is loss! That is, *we begin to manifest the dissolution of those things that no longer work for us, of the untrue that fail to bring genuine peace and joy.* When we remain with our hearts, it can be that we begin to shed the things in the way of our heart's fulfillment. In other words, manifestation oftentimes looks more like defeat and failure, not the fanciful narrative of triumph and glory we may imagine.

The saying is that if you ask God for an amazing life, the first thing that has to happen for most is that the entire foundation of our lives has to be taken down for it to be rebuilt from the ground up. In other words, it's bye-bye to life as we know it!

If we return again and again to our own hearts in this process, we needn't become discouraged at the seeming dissolution of all that we've held to be important. Instead, it's possible to allow for the collapse of what needs collapsing and still find a quiet joy in it all.

And then one day, after a whole lot of relinquishing, we may notice a subtle shift in our perspective. We become aware of a quiet knowing, a sense of trust, a recognition of the truth that all things come. And as we continue to move closer to our hearts, experiences and encounters matching that intimacy with self arise. In turn, neediness, loneliness, disconnection, and any underlying impatience at the unfolding of events begin to fade of their own accord.

Shedding what was no longer true—or perhaps was never so—we come to see is the reason for this new calm, this new knowing. We come to understand that holding onto a falsity in one's life over here and attempting to invite trueness over in another doesn't work, unless one wants to live a compartmentalized, or unintegrated life. And that of course comes with a whole host of issues, all encapsulated by the word *split*.

If your own life feels stuck, look for a cog that may be holding the whole thing in place. It may be a job, a relationship, a house or possession, a habit, an addiction, a withholding of truth, and so on. It's often the thing that offers seeming security and stability but no longer resonates as a hell yes. It's the thing we might find ourselves most attached to without the love. Release that, and you'll watch things flow again.

And if you find yourself unwilling or incapable of letting these things go, you can appreciate any loneliness, neediness, clinginess, and disconnection that arise, as these will supply the fuel for your willingness. Or you can repeatedly come to rest in your heart, and in turn, allow for life itself to conspire to help you.

It may feel unpleasant. Your greatest helpers may appear as the mean, the unkind, and the most unimaginable betrayals. But that's only the appearance. They're in fact your greatest helpers and supporters to flowing again, one day.

Profound gratitude may be the only proper response to such encounters and events.

*Whatever you desire deeply in your heart wants to arrive.* All it takes is the relinquishment of what no longer resonates as true. All of it, one by one. If it doesn't feel scary and profound to let go, there's usually not the relinquishment. And yet when you do, you'll create the opening for what's long been wanting to arrive, finally, to arise.

# 30 The practice of art as a practice in *via negativa*

Back when I wrote poetry and music, I sometimes noted
the tension between an easy choice and not taking it. For
example with music, I'd arrive at a melody that was
catchy, somewhat predictable, and similar to another song
I'd heard but couldn't place. But rather than go with it,
I'd tinker. I'd see if I could push it past the predictable,
while still keeping it pleasurable to the ear. Eventually,
something better, both fresher and closer to my own true
sensitivities would emerge.

I carried this same attitude in writing, whether I was
attempting to write poetry or long essays. I did my best
not to settle for the easy line, or the easy idea—even with
this book and the others. Not seeking difficulty for its
own sake, but for the sake of trueness. (Not sure it's
working but that's the intent!)

I suppose I've been abiding by a general attitude of not
wanting to bore myself, as well as my audience. But it's

also been wonderful training in not taking the easy path, not seeking the expedient solution.

Unbeknownst to me, what's been happening the whole time is I've been zeroing in on my true voice, or something away from the surface and closer to the depths within. I think this one of the primary benefits to upholding a creative/artistic discipline. To create art, we eventually and inevitably learn to become more and more true to an innermost sensitivity. And in our regular attempts to do so, we forge a training ground for practicing the attitude of *via negativa* in choosing trueness over expediency.

# 31 A distinction from welcoming

If we want to be loosey-goosey in our discernment, we can still invite in nice and decent possibilities, but that's what they'll be: nice and decent. Acceptable. They won't necessarily fill us with passion and commitment. They won't wake us with gladness and promise. And that can become our life. Lukewarm. If this is what we want, then we simply welcome in what arrives. If we desire something more, then we take it a step further.

The topic of book 3 in this series was about *welcoming in* what life presented. There's a richness that comes from that as discussed there. But passion is a little different; it takes it a step further. Not only can we experience a sense of inner wealth, we can also experience a sense of intimacy and heartfelt connection to living. This is the natural consequence of practicing greater and deeper discernment in our hearts and minds, and ultimately, in our choices.

In book 3, we learned to refrain from saying no to life *on the basis of our preferences*, and in turn to welcome in what life would offer us, whether we like it or not. And that remains the same. We continue to welcome in what is offered, but we now begin to assert choice—that is, our free will—in what we would choose to move toward ourselves. In other words, book 3 concerns what we allow in—that is, our receptivity—and that's everything. Meanwhile this book is about what we ourselves, proactively, move *toward*. And this requires discernment, not based upon our likes and dislikes, but upon what our hearts speak to us.

In short, as we cultivate the equanimity spoken of in book 3, it frees us to make genuine choice, not based upon ego (i.e., preferences) but upon heartfelt love, truth, and joy, or values that speak to our hearts.

In this way, what touches our hearts may or may not be in sync with our preferences. For example, we may feel called deep within to reach others through writing or speaking, but we may actually *prefer* to stay hidden from others. Book 3 focuses on letting go of the preference for hiding, and this book focuses on learning to listen to the heart's yearning to reach others. Both the letting go of preferences as well as the choosing with discernment are integral elements of a fulfilling life.

## 32 **Approach three:** discerning our dreams from our wants

When I meet someone, I like to ask, *What are your dreams?*

Some come right out with it. *My dream is to go to college and have a career in hospitality and eventually start a family. My dream is to own my business and have enough to buy my parents a nice home. My dream is to start an orphanage in a third-world country.*

Others aren't so clear with it. Maybe it's that their past dreams have been dashed, or they've resigned themselves to the view that dreams are either unrealistic, selfish, and/or pointless.

My own relationship to my dreams has reflected my own relationship to my heart. When I've been out of touch with one, I've been out of touch with the other. And when I've been in touch with one, I'm usually in touch with the other. In this way, I consider uncovering and distinguishing my dreams from my wants as the same as uncovering and distinguishing my heart from whatever social programming I've bought into from my past.

So how do we uncover our dreams?

We do so by relinquishing or slowly letting go of all that isn't our dreams. It's the *via negativa* attitude once again. And yet, the question arises, how do we distinguish those things that aren't our dreams, those wants that we may take as dreams but aren't of the heart? In short, what is the difference between a dream and a want?

I've noted two distinctions:

1.  A want denigrates the present while a dream warms the present. When we're wrapped up in a want, the present moment is lessened. For example, if I live in Los Angeles, but wish I lived in Hawaii instead where the wish is more *of the want* variety, then suddenly, living in Los Angeles becomes less bearable. What *is* becomes diminished through the want. I feel less appreciative of life as it is due to the want.

    On the other hand, if the thought of living in Hawaii is *of the dream* variety, the thought itself infuses the present moment with a warmth, hope, and promise of things to come. Living in Los Angeles becomes more bearable and even enjoyable *because* of the dream. The dream lends the current situation a tenderness of heart.

    In fact, *I've come around to defining the function of a dream as that which enriches the present moment, and this enriching quality, not its actual achievement, as its true fruition.* Dreams lend the current moment with hope and promise in our movement toward their actualization. They do this just in the thought of them, as dreams are of the heart, and so in thinking a dream, we're awakening ourselves to our own hearts.

2.  And this leads to a second distinction that I wrote of a few chapters before, which is that of a patience that accompanies a dream. There isn't the usual frustration and impatience of a want. Instead, there's an inherent patience accompanying dreams because they come with a *knowing* or *trust* around their fruition. This doesn't mean that all dreams come to be; it's that they come with an understanding that what is best regarding the dream is what will come to be. This trust is a hallmark feature of a dream as well as of the heart. The heart naturally trusts while the mind (the center of want) doubts.

So be on the lookout for those longings that enrich the present experience of living, that bring a smile to the face or a tenderness in the breast/chest when they arise in consciousness. They speak of what's in our hearts. They help us to discern the heart's yearnings from the mind's wants.

We can state the same idea in another way: wanting something and feeling insecure that we may not get it, or feeling frustrated that it's not happening fast enough is already the sign of a want. We're already not true. Impatience itself *is* the indication of the surface choice, not a choice arising of the heart but more a compulsion accompanied, many times, by obsession.

In addition to the two "hallmark features" from above, there's also many times a sense that a dream is willed or desired from without, whether from the universe, the people around us, God, whatever. And in turn, the distinction between a yearning arising from within and from without becomes blurred.

## 33 Discouragement: turning back toward the heart

In any pursuit, discouragement can arise as if a thorn in our sides. We can become discouraged from finishing that book or project, or from continuing in a relationship or vocation. We can also become discouraged in the middle of a competitive event, or in argument with a significant other among many other instances of where and how it can appear. We're often taught that it's something to be overcome.

Here, I want to couch discouragement as a positive development, as a useful reminder, as something not to be overcome but as a call to be heeded!

When we look into the etymology of the word (*dis-* ("away") + *cor* ("heart")), we find a hint of its original meaning, as a moving away from the heart. When we become discouraged, we also call it losing heart, but this isn't losing heart as in misplacing and losing track of it, but it's losing heart as in we've been *moving away* from it and thus have lost sight of it.

Discouragement tells us that our attention has been off of what matters, and that if we persist on our current course, we're about to embark on a fruitless journey—fruitless because it will be without our heart, our soul, our truth, our being. It's a call to pull back and to reassess, reconsider, and realign our involvement so that our hearts are back in it. Instead of continuing onward on a circular journey of futility, it's our hearts telling us to come back home, to come back to our truth.

It may mean abandoning our involvement in whatever it was that stirred up the discouragement, whether for a brief or long period.

Mostly, discouragement means that our aim is off. It's an important part of the feedback mechanism within ourselves—our personal GPS, if you will. It tells us that we've lost touch with something important. And so it's a call for recalibration so that we can come back again from the deepest place within ourselves.

If you have a tendency to become discouraged easily, it only means that you have a habit of moving without your heart, or that you tend to spring ahead of your heart. But it also means that you have a wonderfully vocal heart, that your internal GPS is working well! Likewise, if you want to know where you tend to move without your heart, just look for where you easily become discouraged.

Sometimes I become discouraged as a writer. But without fail, what's happening is that my motives for writing have shifted from a heartfelt impulse to explore, learn, compose, create, and express toward an externally-focused attitude of becoming more rigid about my writing habits, bemoaning my slow pace of writing, wanting more readers and income, and on and on this tiresome list proliferates beneath my awareness. My heart could care less about the latter. And yet, it's easy to start doing things for reasons other than the heart's own intrinsic impulse to express its joy (as writing is for me).

So when I become discouraged, it just means I need to reassess why I'm doing this until I remember. Then, showing up to writing becomes less onerous (although it's always hard work and somewhat burdensome for a lazy personality like mine). And as I find myself showing up to it, writing soon begins to happen, and I'm only going along for the ride!

The word relationship derives from the Latin *relationem* (meaning "a returning, a bringing back"). On surface, this seems to suggest that a relationship is that place we return to, again and again. And yet, upon reflection of that fact that *relationem* is a noun whose meaning is "a returning," it might be truer to say that the heart of relationship occurs *in* the returning. That is, *we are in relationship when we're in the act of returning itself.*

In reality, there is no such "thing" as a relationship. It's just a conceptual framework for speaking of how we relate with some other, whether that other is a human, dog, plant, book, nature, and so on. What the etymology of the word suggests is that relationship itself comes alive or *comes to be* in those moments of returning. Not when we're close nor during the parting but in the returning.

In this way, we can think of discouragement as the potential precursor to the returning. It's the signal, as I wrote above, that we've moved away from our hearts. If we learn to heed its call, it reminds us to return, yet again, to our hearts. It becomes the seed, the origin, the beginning of the returning—that is, it becomes the spark that reignites our relationship with our own hearts, thus making it an integral part of the ebb and flow of the one relationship that then shapes all other relationships in our lives.

## 34 Approach four:
## speaking our truth

*A man believes that he is a kernel of corn, and goes to a psychiatrist who, after several treatments, finally convinces him otherwise. He leaves the office relieved, until he runs into a chicken on the street. He turns and runs back, terrified of being eaten and asks the psychiatrist what he should do. The psychiatrist replies, "But why are you afraid? You know you aren't a kernel of corn!" The man replies, "Yes, but does the chicken know?"* —Unknown source.

One way of discerning our hearts is to discern our truth, and sometimes, to speak it. As we do so, we can come truer to our own hearts.

This doesn't mean spouting off every little thought to anyone who will listen. Instead, it means noticing when we want to hide parts of ourselves from ourselves or others, and having the courage for owning and/or expressing that truth instead of hiding it from ourselves and others.

Becoming willing to acknowledge the truth of a situation within ourselves can lead to difficult decisions and actions, while expressing our truth with another can sometimes mean the loss of temporary security or even the relationship itself. But in both cases, we also regain connection to our own being—that is, to our hearts. And in so doing, the relations we do retain can become that much more genuine and supportive of the well-being and happiness of all involved.

On the other hand, if we give in to our fears and fail to recognize and speak our truths, we can end up lonelier, disconnected from others because we're disconnected from ourselves. And yet at the same time, it's exactly this sense of disconnection that can thrust us into situations where we're forced to speak these truths. In this sense, we need only to know what it is we're not speaking. We either share it, or life sometimes forces its hand upon us to do so. (Or else we implode or shut down.) The former is usually less messy, but some of us enjoy messiness until we no longer do. As a friend of mine likes to say, "It's all good" (until it isn't).

In the serenity prayer ("God, grant me the serenity to accept the things I cannot change, the courage to change the things I can, and the wisdom to know the difference."), the second clause cites courage. It's this courage that's required in speaking our truth. *We don't speak it to change the other. We speak it because it asks to be spoken by us.* And whether the other truly hears us or not, whether our words are honored or not isn't the point. The point is in honoring the expression. We can allow for our words to fall where they will, as we're not intent on the outcome but on how truthful we can be. (It's similar to the earlier comments on inhabiting our yearning. It's less about bringing them to actualization and more about allowing for their natural expression.)

As we begin to acknowledge and even speak our truth, we also begin to choose and act from that same place. And as we do so, we begin to draw into our lives those who also live in proximity to their own truth, as such persons will understand and appreciate the courage involved in living and being in this manner. Others who aren't so truthful with themselves may admire us or be uncomfortable around us, and they may also keep a distance, but that's really not our business. Our job becomes to adhere to what we come to know as being true, which isn't a harsh intellectual truth, but the heart's truth. These aren't criticism or attacks upon others. They're our expression of our experience.

And as we give voice to our heart's deepest truths, we slowly come to know the nature of our hearts, which is to come into discernment.

## 35 How we stay speaking our truth

It's one thing to talk about speaking our truths. It's another thing doing it.

The challenge for many of us is that of staying with what's wanting to be expressed from within without teetering over into people-pleasing or denial. It can be easy to *begin* speaking what's true for us, and before we know it, we're watering things down into something much more palatable but less resonant to ourselves and possibly even to the other because (a) we don't want to hurt the other person, (b) we don't want to cause unnecessary conflict, (c) we don't want to deal with conflict, (d) we're afraid of conflict, (e) we suddenly get confused with what we want to say, (f) we want to be accountable for our part in things, and on and on this list (of excuses) goes!

In each of the justifications above, the focus shifts from expressing that which is *within* to somehow concerning ourselves with the *other*. And while this may sound noble and considerate, upon closer examination, we might notice that this isn't exactly what's happening. The shift isn't necessarily to the embodied other—that is, to the actual person in front of us—but it's to the other *as held in our minds.* Our worry isn't about the real other, but it's about the other as we've constructed and conceived in our minds. This is to say that the focus is shifting from within our being, our hearts, our bodies and into our heads. *It's not a shift from within to without, but a shift from our hearts to our heads.*

If this becomes apparent to us, then the solution becomes clear as well. And that's to stay in our bodies as we communicate our truth. We don't go into our heads. Instead, we check in with our bodies, our hearts, our bellies, as we seek out the words wanting to be expressed from there. This is how we stay in our truth.

I once attended a workshop on Eugene Gendlin's work on focusing[3], and one of the things I found was that the experience of communication was much more resonant, and thus clearer, when I stayed in my own body, both as the speaker as well as being the listener. As speaker, I had an anchor that I could return to that kept me out of my head, which is to say that it kept me out of recurrent loops of self-justification and rationalization along with imaginings that may or may not have corresponded to reality. As the listener, I could ground myself as well as help ground the speaker into his/her body as s/he spoke.

In this way, speaking our truth becomes synonymous with grounding ourselves in our bodies and tuning in to what the heart and belly are speaking to us, *and sometimes,* to the other.

---

[3] See *Focusing* (1982) by Eugene Gendlin. One can also learn more by visiting the Focusing Institute at www.focusing.org.

## 36 Honesty

Related to speaking one's truth is honesty, for which the most workable definition I've come across is *preciseness of speech*.

In order to be precise in speech, we have to be paying attention both to our experience and to our words. If someone asks us how we're doing, "I'm fine" isn't particularly precise. Instead, "Overall, I'm doing well, but I have some anxiety about work, and I'm not sure why" is not only more precise, but also, more honest and revealing. It opens up who we are in that moment.

This doesn't mean giving a ten-minute monologue to each question that's asked of us. We can still be brief if that's what's called for. But we can do our best to respond with as much precision as we're able to muster within that brevity.

This precision of attention and expression is a way of allowing others into our experience of living. It's the counter to vagueness, which can keep others on the "outside."[4] In fact, some of us habitually hide behind vague answers to questions. We could be suffering from tremendous self-doubt, but when a close friend asks us how we're doing, we could say, "Not great" or even "Okay." This vagueness can be like a fog that veils what's actually happening, and in turn can act as a buffer to the other from entering into meaningful engagement with us. (Of course, in some close relationships, it might be enough to convey the depths.)

On the other hand, if in an attempt to be precise we answer, "A recent conversation with someone I thought I knew is stirring up doubts about my own perception and judgment of others," this begins to allow the other into our experience. And though not everyone will respond accordingly, for those who are willing and/or able, it becomes an invitation for more meaningful communication and genuine intimacy.

---

[4] Of course, we sometimes consciously choose others to be on the outside.

# 37 A last word on truthfulness

Sometimes I feel out of sync, basically disconnected.

There's one question above all that begins to move things for me back toward discernment, and eventually, to a sense of connectedness. That question is this: *Where in my life or in what way am I not being truthful?*

Usually, asking the question is enough. I already know the answer as soon the question is posed.

So I then begin the work of reconciling who I am in my actions and speech, and who I represent myself to be to myself and others, and with that, the experience of disconnection gradually dissipates of its own, and in turn, my own heart is revealed to me.

## 38 Approach five:
allowing for time to
reveal all things

Sometimes we know in the moment. And other times discernment comes over time. The most vivid version of this can be when we're intimately involved with someone for a long time, only to discover upon parting the true nature of the relationship (and possibly the others' character throughout that involvement).

It's something I noticed as an undergraduate, this sometimes-delayed nature of discernment.

At the time, I involved myself with different groups of friends and acquaintances, but there were two that provided a sharp contrast. One was a group of peers with whom I would generally have a fun time. The other was a group of elders, whose company I found mostly boring, and yet I was drawn to their open and relaxed attitude about life.

One night, after spending some time with the elder group, I was walking to my car alone. The night was quiet and clear, and I was abruptly struck by a feeling of deep peace and ease that would stay with me for days. Further, I felt a sense of promise about my future—something that was uncommon for me at the time. It was nothing anyone said to me. It could have been that the elders were loving me without my knowing. What I realized then was that this was simply a stronger version of how I usually felt after spending time with them. It just took me many months to notice.

I then reflected upon how I felt after spending an evening with my peers. While I liked it, I also couldn't recall a single instance where I came home afterwards with the same feeling of peace and promise within. In fact, the more constant experience was that I would return with a feeling of not wanting to miss out on all the fun I thought everyone was having (or what's now commonly referred to as the fear of missing out (FOMO))! I also remembered the many times I would come back to my studio apartment with a compulsive need to eat, even if I wasn't hungry, as if I were attempting to bury unexpressed anxiety with food.

The distinction was clear. Even though I would have said that I enjoyed spending time with my peers more, I could also now see that I enjoyed and relished *the rest of my life* more so after spending time with the elders.

I then began to scan my mind across many of the relationships in my life, and instead of gauging them by how much I liked the person or their company, I decided I would reconsider these relationships by how I felt about myself and my life 20- 60 minutes after parting from their company. That is, something in me implicitly understood then that my capacity for discerning the true nature of a connection, in the moment, was compromised, likely due to some level of codependence in me, and that the truth of the relationship would become more fully revealed to me through what lingered—the residue, if you will.

What I began to recognize was that in fact the after-effects of an interaction were more indicative of my heart's experience of that interaction. As I began leaning in more toward those relationships that left a greater sense of ease and hope for a more promising future, these qualities of being slowly became my character. And as they became so, the time lag for discerning what was going on underneath an interaction shortened to where that knowing could gradually begin to occur in the moment. That is, true discernment was emerging of itself.

# 39 Choice

The conscious exertion of choice imbued with discernment is the ultimate endpoint of settling and transforming disconnection. True agency, true choice is the gift. Free will, which isn't choice in some egotistical or self-serving way, but the capacity to choose what the universe would ask of us (or anticipates that we choose) is the result. It's the union of oneself with the universe, or God. It's this union, showing up as choice no longer divorced of our hearts, and choice no longer separate from what the cosmos would want for us.

It's not simply the recognition and openness to what arises, but *it's the choosing of that,* not in some intellectual manner, but from our hearts. It's choosing what happens. It's what Byron Katie refers to, no doubt, in the title of her best-selling title, *Loving what is.* When we love what is, we not only are open and accepting of it, but we also seek it with her hearts. It then becomes a dance that blurs the lines between inside and outside, between the yearning of our hearts and the flow of the universe. We soon begin to see, as she says, that things don't happen *to* us, but they happen *for* us.

# 40 Approach six:
## discernment as hearing & listening

When some talk of clarity, they actually mean discernment—that is, they want to separate out the true from false in their thinking. "I want clarity on this situation" can mean that they want to know what's true for them.

But sometimes, clarity can also mean seeing the whole picture, the grand vision. It can mean perspective, as in being able to better contextualize whatever dilemma or issue is at hand.

I'll suggest that the latter—i.e., gaining perspective—is true clarity of *vision*, that is, *seeing* a larger view of the terrain and goal. It's what individuals as well as companies mean when they speak of formulating a personal/corporate *vision* for themselves. This "seeing" is what I spoke of in part two of this series. If you seek the kind of clarity that would help to put things into a larger perspective, then you would do well to go back all the way to book 1 of this series and learn about creating space, from which there can be an openness of being. Once that openness has been cultivated, you can work through the stuck places within your own psyche as described in book 2 until you arrive at genuine perspective and vision (think of it as eating away the blockages into a clearing)!

But if you already have a sense of the overarching perspective and are more interested in discriminating what's true from what's not—a kind of "fine-tuning" or refinement of understanding—then this is the book, and disconnection is the fuel.

In fact, I would suggest the kind of "clarity" associated with discernment is better described as clarity of *hearing* rather than clarity of *seeing*, as hearing clearly is to hear the differences and being able to distinguish, discriminate, and discern, whereas *seeing* clearly is more about perceiving the whole view.

# 41 Coming into us

We take in what we hear.

If we don't like something we're *looking* at, we simply look away or close our eyes. But if we don't like something we're *hearing*, it feels much more invasive.

Whereas seeing seemingly occurs "out there," hearing is often experienced as a "taking in." This taking in allows us to come closer, more intimate with who or what we are receiving. When we look and see, other is separate from self, and yet when we listen, that other's speech (or sound if other is something such as a brook or the wind) enters us. The resulting closeness with other sometimes allows us to move closer to the heart of the matter. In fact, we can't know another very closely unless we are able take some aspect of that other *into* us.

Have you ever noted how hearing and listening can be so much more an intimate act than seeing? When we look upon our love's face or body, there may be admiration, happiness, sweetness, lust, and so on, but how much more intimate is it to hear their sweet whisperings? How much more their tenderly expressed words, utterances, groans and moans reach into us, into our hearts and into our being.

This "coming into" is in the nature of intimacy, and it's intimacy that's synonymous with discernment, for to discern is to arrive at the essence of things. In order to arrive at that innermost aspect, we have to come close, into union with what we want to discern. So we bring them *into* us. We bring the situation *into* us.

## 42 The development of discernment, **approach six** (reprise)

If you consider listening with fine-tuned attention as a metaphor for discernment, it should be clear why detachment is necessary. Think of a typical conversation. To be fully engaged in a lively conversation requires listening.

Suppose you have a habit of either (1) wanting to steer conversations back to topics that you like talking about, such as to yourself, or (2) you often cogitate over what you'll say while the other is talking. Both of these tendencies can be thought of as a lack of detachment, or more an attachment to one's own agenda and ideas. And notice how they get in the way of you truly hearing, not just what the other is saying, but also what may be arising from deeper within. You might still grasp the gist of what the other is sharing, but you're unlikely to tease out the subtler points being expressed. You may also fail to hear a quieter voice from within, which may have helped to deepen the conversation from your side.

If being a good listener is akin to possessing discernment, then not needing to steer a conversation is akin to practicing detachment. If you have no agenda on a conversation, then you're free to listen and take in what's being offered, both from the other as well as from a deeper place within.

One way then to develop detachment, and thus discernment, is to practice listening outwardly and inwardly during conversations. You can try noticing when you start trying to steer the direction of the conversation. If you do, you can simply drop your agenda, and listen. If you feel called to express what's surfacing from within, that too can be expressed of course. But the emphasis is on the listening—that is, even when speaking, it's less about wanting to make a point, and more about allowing for what's showing up from deeper within to speak.

This can become a kind of informal practice of the development of discernment.

# 43 **Approach seven** (the most direct method): listening to the heart

The development of discernment comes down to a simple question: *How do we practice discernment of our own hearts?*

The answer is, *we do so by listening to it.*

This is different from *looking* into our hearts, as if we were seeking something. If we're looking for something, it can lead to impatience in not finding.

Instead, we listen. We enter our hearts and *wait.* There's nothing we're seeking. We simply listen, and if nothing is heard, nothing is heard. We only remain in our hearts, dwelling there, listening to what it might tell us.

*In time,* we begin to hear what it speaks to us.

Many times the heart speaks its own pain.

*What you might find is that the heart has longed to be listened to for a long time, and in some ways, that's all it's longed for. And maybe that's at the heart of what you've ever sought from companionship—to have your own heart (not necessarily your babblings) listened to. You only thought it had to be someone else. But you were there all along. You were the one given the holy task of bearing witness to your own heart.*

Again, this isn't listening *for* something. This isn't listening for guidance. This is listening, as in hearing what our hearts have to tell us, *not for our use*, but because we want to know what it wants to express. Not because we have to do anything with what we hear, but because we understand that our hearts only want to be heard for its own sake, not for our egoistic or sentimental agenda.

As you patiently attend to the task of listening to the heart, you may one day notice a quiet peace where there used to be disconsolate restlessness. With that, there isn't the seeking of relief from disconnection and loneliness since the heart has found its own peace. And maybe that was the connection it sought all along, to be linked to its own intrinsic peace? And in doing so, maybe it can finally, simply *be*.

What *need* is there now for artificial and dissatisfactory connection when a heart simply *is*, at rest and at ease? It requires no manufactured connection because *it's already entwined with all of life simply in its being.* There's nothing that needs to be overlaid on top of such a heart.

It's found its fulfillment in resting unto itself, a feeling of homecoming. And in so doing, others might now be drawn to such a heart since all of us, in one form or another, are seeking to come home to ourselves, to our own hearts. In this way, our heart can now become a beacon for others.

With a heart that is heard, and thus allowed to be, we become less driven by the craving for greater intimacy with another. It's not that one is closed off to it, but there isn't the *need* (or neediness, really, and the craving).

There's nothing "out there" now for the heart to seek. It can rest joyfully and contentedly in its own fulfillment. It can abide in accordance with the adage that happiness is not to be found "out there." Because there isn't the externalized seeking, a knowing arises—a knowing that its own fulfillment comes simply with patient abiding, and because of that, detachment from outcome comes to be.

This is now a heart that can better discern its way through the world. Since it has fewer "external" needs, there isn't a subtle desperation in seeking connection. Others will sense this. They'll either recognize a need to rise up to meeting such a heart, be inspired to doing so, or simply revel together with you with their own heart at ease.

## 44 A few key points in review: different ways of saying the same thing

If we're feeling disconnected, we connect to that. If we're in the dark, we connect to that. We connect to what is.

This journey is about coming into our hearts, which is the same as coming into our truth.

We don't find. We're found. This is the phenomenologically true description of arriving home, of arriving to our hearts. We don't find our hearts. Our hearts arise within our consciousness. Just as we don't make ourselves fall in love. It *happens* to us. It's a being done unto, *grace itself...*

The narrative here is about the interplay between the depths of one's heart and what the universe seeks for us. These two are continually in alignment, and thus, coming into our hearts is the same as entering the flow of the universe. In this way, this is a story of union, of interdependence, or of the disintegration of the conceptual barrier between within and without.

Sometimes we have a knowing. A knowing that something is coming, or that something will happen. There isn't the usual clinging or insecurity. Instead, it's a knowing and a confidence of an inevitability. A key feature of this knowing is detachment. There isn't impatience or frustration at when or how it will happen. The detachment comes because of the knowing, and the knowing can be there only because of the detachment to time-frame and outcome.

Something actionable: Think of doing something, and if you attend to your heart, it can tell you whether it brings happiness or not. Aligning your choices with your heart in this manner can lead to a more heartfelt and easeful bearing. Our bearing then shapes our life. What purpose is there for neediness then?

This is to encourage a re-reading—one could replace truth with an inward beauty, and the same flow of ideas would hold. That is, moving toward our truth is synonymous with moving toward an inward beauty, for what is genuine beauty but a glimpse of something true and truth but a beauty of the mind?

# 45 Final summary

It's a simple journey, from disconnection to utter connection within one's heart to its own peace, and through that peace, with the world around us.

Our job is only to remain listening to the heart, to its yearnings, again and again.

Can you do that?

If not, you can ask for the fuel of loneliness and clinging to be given to you, and you invite it in. *You take it in.*

# 46 Postscript

You've now arrived at the end of this book. I hope that you've come away from it, initially, with greater willingness and courage to face any feelings of disconnection and loneliness you may experience, or be experiencing. Or maybe you've come to recognize the many ways in which distraction supports some degree of disconnection in your life, and you now have greater willingness to let a few of them go?

If you choose to re-read the book (which I do suggest), I do hope that the different manners of cultivating a discerning heart as outlined in the book will begin to show up more so in your life. Please also take a look at my sporadic travel blog, where I offer a more personal version of some of these same ideas at www.yuichihanda.com/middlepath.

In the next book of the series, I will explore the family of mental and emotional states associated with control, competitiveness, and jealousy—and their corresponding gifts.

Also, if you have enjoyed this book in any way, I ask that you consider posting a review of whatever length you feel willing to write. It's encouraging for me to know that others are reading and taking in what I'm offering (or arguing with me!), and also, it lets other potential readers know whether a book might be worth reading or not.

Thank you for your engagement, and I wish you well in the unfolding of all of your dreams.

Yours, yuichi

## The Gifts that Lie Hidden within Difficult Emotions (Part 4): Disconnection and Loneliness

Disclaimer: The information provided herein is for educational and informational purposes only and solely as a self-help tool for your own use. Always seek the advice of your own Medical Provider and/or Mental Health Provider regarding any questions or concerns you have about your specific health or any medications, herbs or supplements you are currently taking and before implementing any recommendations or suggestions from any outside source. Do not disregard medical advice or delay seeking medical advice if necessary. This book is not intended as a substitute for the medical advice of physicians. Do not start or stop taking any medications without speaking to your own Medical Provider or Mental Health Provider. If you have or suspect that you have a medical or mental health problem, contact your own Medical Provider or Mental Health Provider promptly. Although the author and publisher have made every effort to ensure that the information in this book was correct at press time, the author and publisher do not assume and hereby disclaim any liability to any party for any loss, damage, or disruption caused by errors or omissions, whether such errors or omissions result from negligence, accident, or any other cause.

(Besakih Temple, Bali, 2019.)
Yuichi Handa now writes full-time,
part of the time. Or maybe it's
part-time most of the time? Words…
He looks forward to writing the
next book in this series!

Made in the USA
Las Vegas, NV
17 February 2022

44100767R00065